The Fantastic Undersea Life of

JACQUES
COUSTEAU

Dan Yaccarino

Dragonfly Books 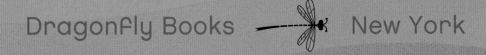 New York

"The sea, once it casts its spell, holds one in its net of wonder forever."
—Jacques-Yves Cousteau

Jacques Cousteau loved the sea.
He spent his whole life exploring it.
The ocean was the most incredible
place he'd ever seen, and he wanted
to share its beauty with the world.

"Man has only to sink beneath the surface and he is free. Buoyed by water, he can fly. . . ."

Growing up in France, little Jacques was a weak and sickly boy. Doctors encouraged him to swim to build up his strength. He discovered that he loved the water.

Jacques also loved to tinker and build all sorts of gadgets.

He saved his money and bought a camera to make his own movies, then took it apart to see how it worked.

When he was a young man, Jacques was badly hurt in a car accident. Doctors told him he would have to wear arm braces for the rest of his life, but he refused to accept this. Just as he had done before, he turned to the sea for strength and swam every day in the Mediterranean.

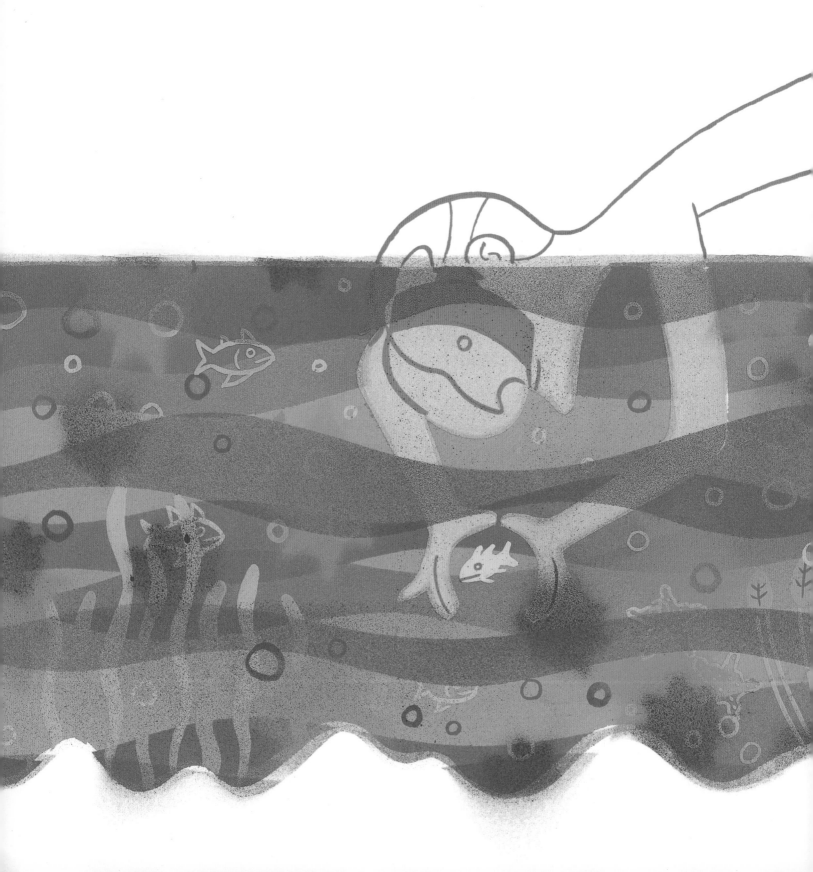

A friend gave him a pair of goggles so that he could see underwater. Those goggles changed his life forever.

"Sometimes we are lucky enough to know that our lives have been changed. It happened to me that summer's day when my eyes opened to the world beneath the surface of the sea."

Cousteau wanted to stay underwater longer to see even more. The diving suits of his day were heavy and bulky. They didn't allow much freedom of movement, and an air hose tethered the diver to a boat.

"Always I rebelled against the limitations imposed by a single breath of air."

So Jacques set about tinkering, fashioning snorkels from things like inner tubes and garden hoses. But they weren't good enough.

Cousteau and his engineer friend Emile Gagnan created a breathing apparatus they called the Aqua-Lung. It was the first machine that would let a diver breathe underwater for long periods of time.

"I flew without wings."

Now Cousteau was free to truly explore.
A silent world opened up to him.

Cousteau wanted to share the amazing beauty of the sea with the world, so he created an airtight cover for his camera. He made lights to illuminate the sea's mysteries, and found ways to film underwater.

"It fascinated me to do something that seemed impossible."

Cousteau bought a boat and turned it into his very own floating research lab and film studio. He sailed his beloved *Calypso* all over the world.

"What is a scientist after all? It is a curious man looking through a keyhole, the keyhole of nature, trying to know what's going on."

Cousteau discovered many treasures in the
Mediterranean Sea. And it was there that he
shot *The Silent World,* the first full-length,
full-color underwater film ever made. It took
the world by storm!

"The best way
to observe a fish
is to become
a fish."

Cousteau's film gave people their first glimpse of the amazing universe under the waves. Everyone loved what they saw as much as Jacques did, and they wanted to see more.

Cousteau's team invented the Diving Saucer, which could hold two people and descend 350 meters into the ocean.

Next came the Sea Flea,
which held one person and
could go down 500 meters.
Cousteau was on a never-
ending quest to go deeper
and learn more.

"We must
move on
deeper."

Cousteau explored the frigid waters of Antarctica and found them teeming with penguins, humpback whales, and squid.

"May this continent, the last explored by humankind, be the first one to be spared by humankind."

Cousteau wanted to see if people could actually *live* underwater. He and his team built a series of underwater labs where people lived and worked for days and weeks at a time.

"I am a believer in today—and tomorrow."

But they found that people need sunlight to live, and so Cousteau's dream of colonizing the ocean was not to be.

Jacques Cousteau was the world's ambassador of the oceans. He produced fifty books, two encyclopedias, and dozens of documentary films.

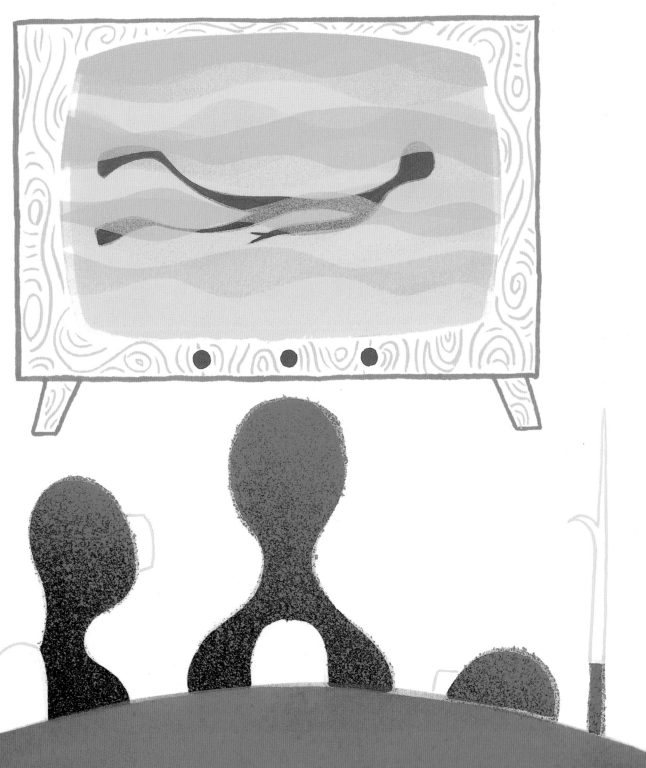

His popular TV series, *The Undersea World of Jacques Cousteau,* brought whales, octopuses, otters, and dolphins right into people's living rooms.

"There was wildlife, untouched, a jungle at the border of the sea."

While exploring off the coast of Australia, Cousteau and his crew saw coral reefs, kelp forests, and sponge gardens. They came face to face with the leafy sea dragon.

When diving in the waters near France,
Cousteau and his crew found a sunken
ship full of wine jars over 2,200 years old!
They tasted the wine. Alas, it was bitter.

The fish off the coast of Africa were friendly and curious and did not swim away. Cousteau was the first human being they had ever seen.

A big grouper adopted the crew while they were filming and mischievously knocked over lights and cameras.

Cousteau and his team explored the world!

"We protect what we love."

But when they went back to the Mediterranean, Cousteau found it had changed. The seas were polluted. Plants and animals were dying. And so the oceans' ambassador became their most important defender. He started the Cousteau Society, which is committed to educating people about ocean life and protecting our seas from pollution.

Jacques Cousteau loved the sea.
He shared its beauty with the
world so that everyone could love
and cherish it too.

"If we were logical,
the future would be
bleak indeed. But we are
more than logical. We are
human beings, and we have
faith, and we have hope,
and we can work."

Some important events in Jacques-Yves Cousteau's life:

• Jacques-Yves Cousteau was born in 1910 in Saint-André-de-Cubzac, France.

• In 1930, Cousteau entered France's naval academy and became an officer in the French navy.

• Cousteau married Simone Melchior in 1937. They would have two sons, Jean-Michel and Philippe.

• During World War II, Cousteau spied for the French Resistance, dressing as an enemy soldier and photographing secret papers. After the war, he was decorated with the Legion of Honor, France's highest award.

• In 1943, Cousteau and Emile Gagnan created the Aqua-Lung.

• In 1950, Cousteau transformed a decommissioned minesweeper into a vessel for oceanic research. The Calypso would be his lab for years to come.

• Cousteau's film The Silent World won the Palme d'Or, the top prize at the Cannes Film Festival, in 1956 and an Academy Award for Best Documentary in 1957.

• Cousteau retired from the navy in 1957 and became director of the Oceanographic Museum of Monaco, and founded the Underseas Research Group at Toulon.

• In 1963, five divers lived in an undersea colony for a month to prove that people can live underwater. This project was called Conshelf II—it was the second of three undersea-living experiments conducted by Cousteau's team.

• Cousteau wrote many books. Two of the most influential, The Living Sea and World Without Sun, were published in 1963 and 1965.

• From 1966 to 1976, Cousteau created the television series The Undersea World of Jacques Cousteau.

• In 1974, he started the Cousteau Society to protect the world's oceans.

• In 1977, Cousteau received the United Nations International Environment Prize. In the same year, his second television series, The Jacques Cousteau Odyssey, premiered.

• In 1979, his son Philippe died in a flying-boat crash.

• The year 1985 saw the launch of Alcyone, a ship powered by energy-saving Turbosails invented by Cousteau's crew.

• Cousteau received the United States Presidential Medal of Freedom in 1985.

• In 1990, his wife, Simone, died.

• Cousteau married Francine Triplet in 1991; they had two children, Diane and Pierre-Yves.

• In 1996, the Calypso sank in Singapore Harbor. Plans are now under way to restore the ship.

• Cousteau died in 1997 at age 87.

Selected Sources for Further Study:

• Cousteau, Jacques Yves. *Jacques Cousteau's* Calypso. New York: H. N. Abrams, 1983.

• Cousteau, Jacques Yves, and James Dugan. *The Living Sea*. New York: Harper & Row, 1963.

• Cousteau, Jacques Yves, and Frédéric Dumas. *The Silent World*. Washington, D.C.: National Geographic Society, 1953, 2004.

• DuTemple, Lesley A. *Jacques Cousteau*. Minneapolis: Lerner Publications, 2000.

• Greene, Carol. *Jacques Cousteau: Man of the Oceans*. Chicago: Children's Press, 1990.

• Munson, Richard. *Cousteau: The Captain and His World*. New York: William Morrow, 1989.

• Reef, Catherine. *Jacques Cousteau: Champion of the Sea*. Frederick, MD: Twenty-First Century Books, 1992.

• www.cousteau.org

Copyright © 2009 by Dan Yaccarino

All rights reserved. Published in the United States by Dragonfly Books, an imprint of Random House Children's Books, a division of Random House, Inc., New York. Originally published in hardcover in the United States by Alfred A. Knopf, an imprint of Random House Children's Books, New York, in 2009. Dragonfly Books with the colophon is a registered trademark of Random House, Inc.

Visit us on the Web! randomhouse.com/kids

Educators and librarians, for a variety of teaching tools, visit us at randomhouse.com/teachers

The Library of Congress has cataloged the hardcover edition of this work as follows:

Yaccarino, Dan.

The fantastic undersea life of Jacques Cousteau / by Dan Yaccarino.

p. cm.

ISBN 978-0-375-85573-3 (trade) — ISBN 978-0-375-95573-0 (lib. bdg.)

[1. Cousteau, Jacques Yves—Juvenile literature. 2. Oceanographers—France—Biography—Juvenile literature.]

I. Title. GC30.C68Y33 2009 551.46092—dc22 [B] 2008004581

ISBN 978-0-375-84470-6 (pbk.)

MANUFACTURED IN CHINA   10 9 8 7   First Dragonfly Books Edition

Random House Children's Books supports the First Amendment and celebrates the right to read.